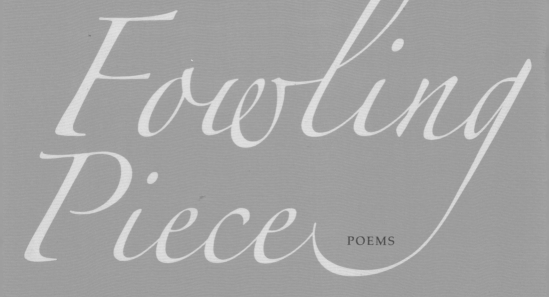

HEIDY STEIDLMAYER

Fowling Piece

POEMS

Fowling Piece

HEIDY STEIDLMAYER

Fowling Piece

POEMS

TRIQUARTERLY BOOKS

NORTHWESTERN UNIVERSITY PRESS

EVANSTON, ILLINOIS

TriQuarterly Books
Northwestern University Press
www.nupress.northwestern.edu

Printed in the United States of America

10 9 8 7 6 5 4 3 2 1

ISBN 978-0-8101-5222-9

Library of Congress Cataloging-in-Publication Data
Steidlmayer, Heidy.
    Fowling piece : poems / Heidy Steidlmayer.
      p. cm.
    Poems, some previously published.
    ISBN 978-0-8101-5222-9 (pbk. : alk. paper)
    I. Title.
PS3619.T4484F69 2011
811.6—dc22

2011015569

∞ The paper used in this publication meets the minimum requirements of the American National Standard for Information Sciences—Permanence of Paper for Printed Library Materials, ANSI Z39.48-1992.

For Eleanor
and for Mary

CONTENTS

Acknowledgments   *ix*

I Say So Long to the Hedge Rider   *3*

Knife-Sharpener's Song   *4*

Poverty   *5*

Fowling Piece   *6*

Figures   *7*

Heartbreak   *10*

Couples   *11*

The Oracle   *13*

Baptism   *14*

Confessional   *15*

Wood Splitting   *17*

Bede on Moonlight   *18*

Divination by Runes   *19*

Taxonomy of Grief   *20*

Agonal   *21*

Potter's Field   *22*

Talking with the Dead   *26*

Short Shrift   *27*

Charon Reconsiders   *28*

Callisto   *29*

Limbo   *30*

Concordance   *31*

Death Outside of Alpine, Texas   *32*

Stars in a Field   *33*

Pulling Up the Lawn Mushrooms 35

The Onion 36

The Entomology Exhibit 37

The Stentor 38

Sundays at the Lepidoptera Exhibit 40

Saint Elias in the Whirlwind 41

The Martyrdom of Saint Bartholomew 42

Relics 43

In the Surgery Bay 44

The Mask 45

Woman in the ICU 46

Resonance 47

Interpreting the Films 48

Riptide 49

The Scan 50

The Doll 51

Intensive Care 52

The Eye Patch 53

Scree 54

Delivery 55

Fairy Tale 56

The Visit 57

The X-Ray 58

Three Daughters 59

The Coracle 60

∽

Scylla 62

Charybdis 63

Notes 65

ACKNOWLEDGMENTS

Grateful acknowledgment is made to the editors of the following publications where these poems and parts of poems first appeared, some in slightly different versions:

Calyx: "In the Surgery Bay" and "Woman in the ICU"

Humanitas: "Wishbone" and "Orrery"

Literary Imagination: "Limbo"

Michigan Quarterly Review: "The Stentor" and "Interpreting the Films"

Ploughshares: "Charon Reconsiders" and "The Oracle"

Poetry: "Riptide," "Knife-Sharpener's Song," "Confessional," "Poverty," "Figure Eight," "Circles," "Talking with the Dead," "I Say So Long to the Hedge Rider," "Scree," "Couples," "Fowling Piece," "Thistles," "Arrival," and "The X-Ray"

River City: "Sundays at the Lepidoptera Exhibit," "Taxonomy of Grief," "Scylla" and "Charybdis" (originally as "Two Scenes of Unresolved Anger"), "Callisto," "Burying the Peacock," "Fabliau," "Baptism," "Concordance," and "Agonal"

Suisun Valley Review: "Burying the Cricket"

TriQuarterly: "Cutlery," "Wood Splitting," "Clothesline," "Turnstile," and "Heartbreak"

"Riptide" was reprinted by *Poetry Daily.*

"Knife-Sharpener's Song" was reprinted in *Poems, Poets, Poetry: An Introduction and Anthology,* by Helen Vendler (Bedford/St. Martin's, 2002).

"I Say So Long to the Hedge Rider," "Scree," and "Couples" were awarded the J. Howard and Barbara M. J. Wood Prize from *Poetry* magazine.

I am grateful for a 2009 Writers' Award from the Rona Jaffe Foundation and for an AWP WC&C Scholarship, which allowed me to complete this manuscript.

I would like to thank Eleanor Wilner, Mary Kinzie, Reginald Gibbons, Linda Gregerson, Ellen Bryant Voigt, Catherine Barnett, Debra Allbery, and my family.

Fowling Piece

I Say So Long to the Hedge Rider

Hey, edge stepper carrying your bag
of quicklime and larks, I thought you'd gone,
hitched your sad self to some old words
like hither and ell, but here you come
tramping through the half-light of the forest
like an idea that is only good on paper.
So here we are at the crossroads—
with each way so dismal, so embolismal,
how will I ever find the curbstone, the term?

Never mind. You are just the ghost
of myself that I will soon be rid of—
I am sending you away, stripped to
your weeds, to your oh-dear in the hallway,
to the series of unfortunate events
that has left me in this darkness
riding the bird cherry and the haw.

Knife-Sharpener's Song

I said no word of her to him,
nor he of her to me, *oh yes.*

We sharpened down the sliding

hour the knives wooled thick
with rust, *oh yes;* the days grew

small and wider, stripping

words down to their edge—
cutthroat, flashy, without a flaw—

what he did to me, *oh yes.*

Turn by turn, those knives of hers
shone quietly aware, *oh yes,*

not I but she would be the one

he carefully undressed—
but he said no word of her to me

nor I to him of us, *oh yes.*

Poverty

No stone field flowers
for love of you, so walk

faster than the fear that
follows you like footprints,
they repeat as you repeat
words until they form
a prayer, let the sun beat
down its fat old heart,
bring another day to its knees—

there is nothing left
to carry but your voice.

Fowling Piece

The pull of guns I understand,
my father taught me hand on hand
how death is. Life asserts.
(Best take it like a man.)

I shot a dove, the common sort
and mourned not life but life so short
that gazed from death as if unhurt.
And I had nothing to report.

Figures

Orrery

To my mind, this mad contraption
sprang from the lonely
hope of knowing planets.

Sad amplitudes of clocky junk
crank moons and tiny globes of granite.

The ratchets interlock like asterisks
to star this, star the flying
planets I have made—and watch,

this one moves retrograde.

Circles

Because it is late
and a man's white shirts
gleam as if frozen,
the woman ironing
dreams of skating in circles,
on edge, leaning in.
Always there are more shirts
before her skating away.
If she is not careful, she will
scorch them as she glides the quiet
length of an untouched lake.

Yes, she thinks, *circles*
eased across the icy surface—
as she presses each crease
breathless, to nothing—
the effort both final and silent.

Figure Eight

Score and torsion
cut from the cold
origin of figures.

Flat maps of planets
follow the slow
going of steel—lines

lengthen to pure
curve—O my arctic
orbiting, end

in universe,
carve from the frozen
hour a far

star of practice,
mark the stark polarity
of one become one

with the dark
rink of eternal morning
where infinity

stands its only skater—
a wobbler tracing great
stases of ice beyond

this wintry affinity.

Turnstile

Turnstiles add, subtract
fractions. A man halved
from the hips down turns

out fine. He still feels

her chill arms lock like handlebars
at his ordinary touch.
That's why he comes around.

Heartbreak

That windows without breaking
promise the sky to sparrows,
shows in a heartbeat how
sorrow is the slowest teacher,
and why, falling for stories
of sparrows untouched by storms,
I'm crestfallen when I can't help
but press my ear hard to your chest,
hear something like your heart
protest too much this death—
so little to do with us.

Couples

Cutlery

Midnight, the knives throw
shadows with showy precision
through my hesitant silhouette.

Old umbrage has brought me here,
unharmed, near missed, where
the thrown blade was your own,
untoward and very fast.

Couples

Even at odds, we manage to make
two live cheaply as one.

It's not hard, by halves, to scrimp—
save when the want splits

the difference of our bodies
as if passion were thrift.

Fabliau

In cahoots only here
for a holiday, he tied me
slick-backed, soft-hackled flies.

Wading lovely on the lam,
catch-as-catch-can, O he horsed
them in so pretty. I tangled my line
in trees and he undid me,
shiny fingered, all allure.

Clothesline

A delicate line of questioning:
ask me if my emptiness equals all
your clothes, if the light shows
through your thinnest shirt
to hurt, or if the wind blows
your darks from the line by design
sad, how they hold your shape
enough to say enough for me
to follow or let go, enough.
Yes and no, I was better for it.

Wishbone

We pick sides, polar—
the pull, unspoken.

Division, it's a start.
Togetherness but a token

to wish for the better
part of something broken.

The Oracle

I see the lion as the lion
sees the girl he slowly
devours in a silent film—

a flash of sun-torn flesh—

before the vision fades.
How foolish she was to wander
the woods alone, forgetting

the warnings, the memory

she had of herself before
the woods became a thought
from which the lion leapt,

parting the darkened grasses

with the quiet sunlight
of a god. What rough tongue
takes out its want as she watches

herself wander into the woods

again—and again it happens;
she looks back, sees
the lion like the lion—

and another devouring.

Baptism

Hungering in ropes
of wonder and sigh,
the hills head off

like horses to the slough
and trough of sea—
even the waves drag,

trundling their bundles
of salt-ripe sea grapes
as the wash-in, wash-out

thrash of sloppy
wrappers, gull feathers,
and fish guts

equally reaches
an afterlife—
the time that waits

beyond what's left
of this stranded eternity,
as people thin

and clear, blown
from the near shore
and the old radiance.

Confessional

Each time I think
        no more evil-
   thinking thoughts, they

accrue to my soul's
        tally
   as grillwork, ironwork

work to conceal
        God's right hand
   in darkness, a man

who would have me
        bitter as Lot's
   wife looking back

at the past
        returning . . .
   how can you absolve

salt, that sin
        of the flesh
   made weak with another's

yearning, would you
        fault
   the one she turned

from for staring
        stolidly
    away . . . should

the good Lord
        preserve
   and keep us in this

life, my father-
        confessor, almoner,
   who shall be spared . . .

Wood Splitting

The maul recalls itself
to itself with a keen
fury that knows no master—
not I, nor the haft
remember to remember
my fear as the past rears
up from behind, reminds
of the blow that will come
down to silence and splitting
cry. What have I?

Bede on Moonlight

He gazed at the moon for years,
the acres and perches of that vast landscape
stranger than he imagined, throwing
its orb over the earthen darkness of a lake
or hanging tumescent in a sky
of incalculable geometries,
crescent glowing flat "like a ship"—
oracular sails from northern flanks
betokening whirlwinds of storm.
Perhaps he looked up at the shifting
shape of clouds or other omens
for the elisions of a drifted body
as he continued (*kyrie eleison*)
on his fluctuating course,
length and brevity fixed in the ether
dissolving as he slowly went on.

Divination by Runes

wolf in forest; sea-fire; serpent-path; gold . . .

great the claw of the hawk; adorner of ships . . .

fallow-hilted; flakes of metal; snow-wound;
weeping of clouds; ice . . .

broad bridge; bark of rivers; roof of wave; sharpest birds . . .

greenest of winter trees; gallows; bent bow;
brittle iron; giant of the arrow . . .

death; corpse-frost; pale skiff; knife . . .

rust, snake-husk, salt-cry; leavings of wolf . . .

Taxonomy of Grief

gray-bitten by sea salt (halted, subaltern), beaten by the damp, ox-tongued heat; operatic vowels (owls, voles, deer) hidden in the woolly everlasting; hares chased (erased) by the moon's vestal stare; bears (fears, near) in the forest; (chorus) O nunlike abundance, O oriole and ember (remember?)

      that fast, that alarm, that harm

               trembling (dissembling) in flare—

words that eat dogbane in the woods

        and collapse

             (hum of wasps)

Agonal

innumerable   inoperable   undoable   unstoppable

hearts   hardening   like porphyry   orphrey   empurpled

with orphics   O faience   the radiance   breaths

resisting   the gift   & the scientific   prophetic   terrific

red tide   revising   the easing

& her side   a widening   gasping   chiasmus   of phosphors

collapsing   let it happen   the rafters   unfasten

miasmas   of sea lettuce   & ash   reducing

her thereness   to bear grass   or moss

& her hair   & my hand

in the enfolding

Potter's Field

1

I am finding Francesca,
father's father's mother, more
difficult than her photograph.

Before the war
Francesca had many horses.

She pretends to ride one
in the cracked light of Francesca,
young and on horseback.

In truth, she fears them.

How the picture lies:
Francesca astride

a jade troubled in harness—
the only photo I have left.

See. Francesca unafraid.

2

Great Francesca
please stop speaking—

now, look at the fine photo
your son has taken of Francesca
fearless on horseback.

No, your son is not dead
of trampling but of the cough—

Anton! Anton! Qui va là?

Someone remove this woman.
[Francesca is thrice removed.]

And everything was taken.

3

*ekwos. eoh. equine.
*khorsaz. ross. horse.

Blancas, the white ones.
Charos, the black one.

Daguerreotype: a type of war.

Anton,   my tamer of horses.
Francesca,   lightwritten—

Hippolyta.   potable.   phosphor.

Harness   and caparison:
entrails   and harns—

patois: a trampling down.

what.   falls.   off.
you.   me.   anton.

Equus caballus.
haruspex.

4

Francesca, if a young girl comes
begging sugar

for her mare, don't answer.
Say to her *cauchemar,*
dismiss her as nightmare—

it is she you should fear.
She speaks French

but curses in Latin—

delenda est Carthago!

She is young enough to have loved
Anton before he was not
trampled and got the cough.

Francesca, the mare was never there.
Francesca, poor in horses.

Talking with the Dead

To consider the shape your breath takes
in the sudden chill of my imaginings: you,

alive again, shouting down the pitch
and yaw of the city's stubborn snowplows—

a sound so real I could touch it before
it dissolved into intimations of mist;

to admit when I see your face in strangers
lit by the half-light of the late train,

I want to ask where you are headed,
if your silence should tell me you are

listening to what I've left unsaid;
to say in those last weeks of long illness

I watched your every sentence soften
like a worn sheet *are you listening, are you . . .*

to talk to you again; to tell you *I am;*
to fill the room's starched emptiness

with a voice that answers to no one.

Short Shrift

From the cliff
face of contrition,
I am throwing stones—

calx, gneiss, bits
of mica schist—
long, long

the list goes on,
a tinny litany
of sins.

O slow rococo,
O mean smithereens,
how can you break

faith and tell
of a life more far
flung commanding?

Charon Reconsiders

He almost pitied them, those buried
with no fare, as he sifted through the sand
of their names and singled out the shades
who would be granted no passage. Their breath
was all cold-packed earth and mossy hush.
How many coins he had now—the wake
turned up their light when he fingered them.
He tallied up how many, how much,
touched the insignia of emperors, kings—
he could taste the metal in his mouth like stars.
Often as he left shore, he thought he might
take one or two, be they pauper or thief,
and offer what fate could not afford them.
But once he ferried the rest to their arrival,
he went back to his black calculations.

Callisto

Cynosure of all
eyes, did he
rise in a hood of bees

and throw off

his otherness?
It is useless to
question the gods

in their old circuity,

but tell me,
starry warriors,
lusty swaggerers,

and I will suffer

your stale exhalations
of ether, I will rise
to darkness—

the poplars, that youth

in the distance—
tell me,
what have they done

with my son.

Limbo

Because there is nothing there *is* that is not
worth dying for, we wait until our bodies take on

the stubborn musculature of sculpture, feel

from where form, like everything fixed, gives
off a kind of grief. So many malingerers!

What faith would suffer us? All night we sleep

the sleep of blindness: bright and isolate,
waiting to wake from dreams that seem no more

than a cold draft—what happens—when another

soul passes. Even the gods were like goods
we could not take with us: sentimental, sad—

they begged us. We left them for others.

Concordance

for the maid is not dead, but sleepeth
for the man is not dead: why troubleth

his brother is dead, and he is left
and his brother is dead, and he alone is

if a thief be smitten that he die
shall wash with water that he die not

the beggar died and was carried by
the rich man died and was buried

signifying what death he should die
lighteth upon his neighbor, that he die

and we shall die without redemption
that we could love without redemption

and as touching the dead, that they rise
bearing about in the body the dying of

Death Outside of Alpine, Texas

Cloaked in goldenweed he arrived
in the canyon's violently changing colors,
chess grass draining into a valley
of clay flats and blackened rabbitbrush.

When the manzanita was flowering
he became imperial as the twisted bark
of that red shrub.

                    Gravel flung in nets
by the wet roadside, a staggered
procession of riders shouldering past.

His body held like light over a last curve.

Stars in a Field

Thistles

stand as clocks fully struck
in fields of fading flowers—
when the fires of summer come
they will gather up the hours
of rains past, frost endured

and famished stalks in full gale
that begin their telling once
all forms of telling fail

Burying the Peacock

Now that there is one less throat
loosing superstitious cries,
the evil-eyed other peacocks vie
in a bright clash, hissing
and striking their likenesses.
Beyond them, a full moon hammers
fields into intaglios of loosestrife,
and what began with a dog's bark
ends with an armful of iridescent death.
We cross ourselves and hurry home.

Burying the Cricket

Chirp infinitely now
on your arid bed of silences,
doll in a tiny white box.

My husband mock-solemn
digging with a child's trowel:
yea, though we walk through the valley
before I said stop saying that

and the hole going deeper,
my daughters throwing
dandelions in, one two three—
then the loose dirt top,
and we all walked quickly away
into a wind that seemed
to be coming from our house.

That night I dreamt a cat
was digging you up like a fallen bird
and when I turned to stop it
from happening I vanished.

Arrival

Midwinter, the crows take
their darkness out on day.
A thin rain falls and breaks.
I wonder at the way

the oaks unravel here
(and travel word of mouth)
another year.
Not going, I go south.

Pulling Up the Lawn Mushrooms

My dreams fill with their fruiting bodies
floating across the front yard—
swathes of young, sublunar forms,
some inchoate with age over papery lamellae,
the empurpled, mottled gills.
The spores leave black smudges
on my fingers when I touch
beneath their crepe-lined caps,
so I pluck each growth by the stipe,
cream-white and silky shining
like a tether to another world.
Do not think them weary in their slump;
even the small ones lift long throats from the thatch
and whisper a thousand assurances.

The Onion

For Eleanor

The early layers tough and leathery
like the peel, color going slowly yellow

where roan skin flecks the sleep-encowled whole
cold from the refrigerator bin,

skin wanting to stick to it, milky juices making for
a biting smell in the eyes, inside

the cut white sinewy cuffs of sleevelike material stretching
across in paper-thin layers, the layers

alive, give off of themselves one by one
as they ring from the center like a bell

and the center is opened
to a green shoot already growing in its dark.

The Entomology Exhibit

Deep in his ester of acetic acid,
the Chinese mantid wilts
facedown to the white backing
that suspends his closest
neighbor, the giant click beetle.

With his octagonal head
bent inwards, I think he is reading
an ancient Sumerian text
in which he rises from the froth
of the ootheca and transcends

himself from the beginning—
like the metallic cuckoo wasps slowly
curving into schwa, the rusty
hasps of the fruit beetle unfolding
such shiny elytra.

The Stentor

Trumpet-
	shaped,
caught in the clear bowl
	of a three-day-old

hay culture, it floats
	on the cool bilge
of its depression slide.
	Billions of years

evolving from some
	non-light-loving
flagellated ancestor, the cell
	glides over to a small

suspension mixed
	with Congo red
stain, its brushlike
	cirri drawing bits

inward as it swims,
	shifting and sampling
the damp offering under
	magnification of 400x.

Reflected in my eye,
	it yawns like the hood
of an old Victrola, bronze
	voice reliving the record

of the triumphant
        dawn of heterotrophs,
when from the lowest
    kingdom they came

in bleary greens and blues
        to be one with
these complex and beautiful
    animalcules that rise

out of silence
        like visions of our invisible
yearning to see first
    things firsthand.

Sundays at the Lepidoptera Exhibit

Rows of imagoes underpin the stillness.

With the invisible symmetry
        of the beatitudes,
        Boisduval's Yellow is visibly

transformed. Even the moths
        possess a momentary gift for epiphany:

night-anointed, deathly emblems of earthly

infatuation, they freight each lamp
        with the last weight
        of candle and cerement.

Who can say what passion transfixes us?

Or why thick ropes
        guard the dais of special acquisitions,

                where the empyrean opens
    itself to nothingness

and a dying line of Lesser Purple Emperors

        receives us.

Saint Elias in the Whirlwind

What to make of
the strange glint of volcanic
horses pulling the sun

to him, the years
falling back like waters
struck with a cloak

and oh the sky riding.

The Martyrdom of Saint Bartholomew

Less supple than the saint,
less permeable to twilight and penumbra,
Ribera's flayer turns to the viewer.
Grinning, he does not decompose
or discolor, his hand does not dissolve
under the influence of shadow
at the pellucid ankle, his atrocity
is not avoided by the lyric
precision of his layered coloring—
and nothing is so peculiar to him
as certain notes of furious red.

Relics

Saint Anne's wrist sunk
in anchored calm, divining
its million fountains
from a single knobby scintilla—

compass of God, bear
this brief body,

the sap of unction, an oddment,
some flinders, the crumbling
blood of Saint Januarius
flickering in its ampoule.

In the Surgery Bay

Eight of us anchored to slabs of cloud
the inhabitants of a pond brought to the surface

in the bed across from my left foot

a man's voice unraveling
his heart
his wife mowing the lawn now
how far his scar would go

the anesthesiologist, her faded countenance
as far away as a giant

my husband beside my bed, his face
as if I had just fallen from one of his branches

The Mask

CyberKnife radiation mask, Stanford

Meshed to my face in cloud work,
it throws a net of blueness over the room

where techs pass like cows, huge
and moon-white near my chin.

I am wearing this blue veil
to show my part in revealing

I've been touched more than once
by an invisible light.

Or so I tell myself. Who knows?
I may be tethered to nothing,

holding the great sea crushed inside a turtle,
the sky leaking from a thousand holes—

or I've fallen in the snow.

Woman in the ICU

Propped up in bed,
my roommate is safe
in the folds of her coma—
she cannot say a word
until she knits eleven
shirts of nettles
for her enchanted brothers.
Three times a day, the nurses
lean into her face
with flashlights and shout,
Can you hear me?
Blink if you can hear me.
But the woman
has gone into herself
like a cottage and the doctors
are swans who surround her,
their dark rustlings
breaking the spell.

Resonance

In the MRI chamber

Faceup in my drawer beneath
elves hammering their bright work
and the down-hard, down-hard of rocks
flung into a ginny, I calculate
the length of a core sample,
wondering who is knocking on my door.
Midway I am conveyed from within,
the parsing of thought into layers,
all thin cuts, my sagittal views.
Once I tasted the unfortunate
tang of someone else's sweat
before going back in. The walls
are round like a church.
Upstairs, a rocking chair is broken,
a coin is tripping down a drain.
More muffled than nonsound, snow
melting, I am rolling out
like a new year. Is this a time capsule—
have they found me intact?
I emerge daub-white, an aubade.

Interpreting the Films

Here I am hunched over another
impression of the brain with its wads
of flat batting and weird yarn, thinking how
can I read these films without a light board—
me, foolishly holding each chronic image up
against the screen door in the kitchen,
my brain's blank cauliflowers over and over,
twenty tiny brain images per page, twenty-five
films, brain, brain, brain—and there
in the center, what everyone is talking about
(itself looking like nothing to talk about),
a shape like one of my daughter's plastic blocks
stuck in the thick of it all, wedged right in the fat
bulb of breathing and bath time and bringing
in the weekend groceries and so I wake
at two A.M. with my films pressed to the side
of a fish that turns in an instant and is gone.

Riptide

The sea gives rise
to a tide of jeremiads,

the *why-me* waves
all sentiment and gush,
go their felo-de-se

way and die sighing
sandy inamoratas
of cant. Who cares

who listens—

not *God,* the tall power
boat, tiny and at sea,

nor the squat tug
lugging its ugly embargo—

but the fat beached fish,

repeating bad tidings
like a line

why go on

while the breakers
break one borne bright
out of foam

and come to nothing.

The Scan

Light sculpts from liquid shadow
a strange echolalic interior,
brain on brain, the blackened sinuses
answering like owls
and I am imagined
in layers of tissue murkily formed,
a gray sheepfold pebbling the dark film
as nonimage annihilates to noise, techs
on the portico regarding
a face in half cloak, in oak leaves, rising
from aura to corona to flare
and the salt become broth still coming
at the back of my throat that brings the whole
to gloriole before it grows
beyond knowing.

The Doll

Pocket of silence, your breath comes from behind a mirror
cold and strange as outer space,

in your eyes a dead reflection of a fixed point, mouth
closed to the secrets of being one

who stares from a high shelf like a dish—your gaze
glazing over miles,

before it fills the room like moonlight or a sunken lake.

Intensive Care

For days I waited for her,
and when she appeared
her face gave its pale moon
to the corner of my bed.
She controlled darkness
and I felt her tall
voice as faraway lights
in a shifting path to the door.

Once I saw her swimming
toward me in a pool of white,
her hands arranging a square
of gardens near the window—
that was the day she pulled
my family like a curtain
and her body's slow blur
came upon me like a town.

The Eye Patch

Here's where I start
to collapse in on myself, pulling
galaxies as I go, a few huge
stars, how they swirl
before they're sucked in

to the hole that has become my eye,
to the nothing that now wants everything
that has become my eye—
the blackness of the patch tricking
my palsied eye into not-seeing as it sees
in the round sea of its dark cup:
the mind in its weedy prominence
opening like a terrible mouth.

Scree

I have seen the arrested
shrub inform the crag with grief.
Lichens crust the rocks with red.
Thorns punctuate the leaf.

Sorrow is not a desert
where one endures the other—
but footing lost and halting
step. And then another.

Delivery

You lived your first hour
afloat in the thin holms
of your ghost basket,
no one to gather you in
but those whose job it was
to push air through a cloud
and to read your foot's foam cuff
for oxygen levels.

I read that they dragged you
from the dark like a sea creature
and set you among babies
missing things like yourself—
kidneys or a piece of heart—
and that you flourished
without me.

Fairy Tale

I want to hide you in a rice grain,
a turnip seed, a magic bean. Imagine!
that I should quicken you, when stories
abound with children who lose
their mother (mothers taken
to sickbeds, mothers drinking
the wrong potion, mothers
dying at the cusp of the sea).
Oh there are moments, my limpet,
my trumpeting swan, I would turn
you back into the blissful instant
before the round hour of your making.
Yesterday would be a flower
you would never visit,
and when we came to the bridge
where we must part—you would not
remember me. I would let you go.

The Visit

On the fifth day, I watch the nurses wheel
my daughter down the white tile.

They whisper together in the doorway
before they look at me sadly like a broken vase.

One lifts my daughter from her clear box
and explains her like a country with too many borders.

A cloth nest is placed in my right arm
while I lie there vaguely, unable to mother her—

she is an ocean away, her small body drifts
into an arctic sleep, she does not know me.

I am useless to her, less than a photograph.
The sunlight through the window convinces

the floor with just one square of normalcy
that the stilted visit is over.

The nurse hands me a pair of footprints
on a big pink card. The dark

impressions haunt me like those of a rabbit.
When they reach the door, the nurses watch my face

as if it will soon go under, the last of a sunset.

The X-Ray

Mornings, the body's old
winter monochrome gives
its image of extraordinary cold
to a million hives—

I could imagine a *lanthorn*
as it swallows its strange light and gleams
from within as if reborn
when the bees come.

Three Daughters

1. Movement

Before my youngest daughter learned
to walk she dreamed for months
that she was walking, her legs ticking
up to some dark room of her being
before she paused, having entered.

2. Dressing

I am pulling a blue turtleneck
on my second daughter,
her head comes up and out
as if she were rising from a drain.

She looks at me in relief and says,
I was gone.

3. Before Bed

My oldest daughter clings to me,
her arms pulling me down like she is drowning.

I will never let you go she says as she lets go.

The Coracle

I set you adrift in withies and pitch,
stripped of all sign I would know by,
cradled in oxskin, nursed by the gorse,
the wind dissolving your cries.

A bird on the mountain, a cork
to the sea, a far-off story of shore—
you float the salt-dark, a speck
vanishing the moment it's more.

Scylla

I marvel at the lean
agency of ships—
tall sloops cutting
the cold elegance
of perfect silence
while winds dim
to a dead gleam.
Some have heard
my dogs, shallow in
the hearts of them,
sound a warning
either too suddenly
or too late, snakes
touching all there is.
You would think
the sea was blind
to me as I stare out,
deaf to the dull
pull of waters that
promise, if not love,
then love or nothing.

Charybdis

I am the crepe de chine of Paris green, rauwolfia, and atropine, I am the shapeless
    keeper,
        the restless sleeper, the jeofail

of sea-change fictions, I am the desuetude, the nudity, the unanswered cry of *ubi*
    sunt, I am
        the pharaoh ant, the unmet want, the vatic O

and armchair throw, I am the malediction, the contradiction, the hollow laugh of
    shell and call, I am the first refusal,

the worst reprisal, the life you haven't lived in years, I am the haymaker, the
    trumpet
        creeper, the desperation rising daily in swales,

I am the swan's road, the oxgoad, the eye of the Ouroboros, I am the ur-version,
    the cold
        vision, that old *either-or* rearing out of

the offing, I am the long-robed arrival of self—an *adieu* in passage—crowned
    with each small salt conclusion

NOTES

"Knife-Sharpener's Song" begins on a variation of two lines that open Stevie Smith's poem "Nor We of Her to Him."

"The Martyrdom of Saint Bartholomew" was inspired, in part, by an encyclopedia entry on Jusepe de Ribera, s.v. "Ribera, Jusepe de" (by Louis Gillet), *The Catholic Encyclopedia,* http://www.newadvent.org/cathen/13031b.htm.